P9-EED-444

GALAXY OF SUPERSTARS

Ben Affleck

Backstreet Boys

Garth Brooks

Mariah Carey

Cameron Diaz

Leonardo DiCaprio

Tom Hanks

Hanson

Jennifer Love Hewitt

Lauryn Hill

Ewan McGregor

Mike Myers

'N Sync

LeAnn Rimes

Britney Spears

Spice Girls

Jonathan Taylor Thomas

Venus Williams

CHELSEA HOUSE PUBLISHERS

GALAXY OF SUPERSTARS

Mariah Carey

Sam Wellman

CHELSEA HOUSE PUBLISHERS
Philadelphia

Frontis: *Mariah Carey with two of her American Music awards. Her dazzling singing style has earned her over a dozen major music awards since 1990.*

Produced by
21st Century Publishing and Communications, Inc.
New York, New York
http://www.21cpc.com

CHELSEA HOUSE PUBLISHERS

Editor in Chief: Stephen Reginald
Managing Editor: James D. Gallagher
Production Manager: Pamela Loos
Art Director: Sara Davis
Director of Photography: Judy L. Hasday
Senior Production Editor: LeeAnne Gelletly
Publishing Coordinator: James McAvoy
Contributing Editor: Anne Hill
Cover Designer: Terry Mallon

Front Cover Photo: Anthony Dixon/London Features Int'l
Back Cover Photo: Gary Merrin/London Features Int'l

The Chelsea House World Wide Web address is
http://www.chelseahouse.com

First Printing

1 3 5 7 9 8 6 4 2

Library of Congress Cataloging-in-Publication Data

Wellman, Sam.
   Mariah Carey / Sam Wellman.
   64 p. cm. – (Galaxy of superstars)
   Includes bibliographical references and index.
   Summary: Presents a biography of one of the best-selling recording artists of
the 1990s, whose vocal styles are drawn from gospel and rhythm and blues.
   ISBN 0-7910-5233-8 (hc); ISBN 0-7910-5333-4 (pb)
   1. Carey, Mariah—Juvenile literature. 2. Singers—United States—Biography—
Juvenile literature. [1. Carey, Mariah. 2. Singers. 3. Women—Biography]
I. Title. II. Series.
ML3930.C257W45   1999
782.42164'092—dc21
[b]   99—31804
                                                              CIP
                                                               AC

CONTENTS

1

DAZZLING DIVAS

On the Tuesday evening of April 14, 1998, something very special began for pop singer Mariah Carey. She and four other women in glitzy evening gowns waited backstage at the Beacon Theater in New York City. They were billed as the five "divas," who would perform a concert that evening called "Divas Live." Diva is an Italian word for goddess, and these five divas were Mariah, Aretha Franklin, Celine Dion, Gloria Estefan, and Shania Twain. Combined, the five had recorded over two dozen number-one hits, won nearly two dozen Grammy awards, and sold over 200 million albums. Describing these five singers as divas was not an exaggeration. They were adored by fans the world over.

Executive producer of "Divas Live," Lauren Zalaznick, was overjoyed. "It's uncanny. It's wacky," she bubbled. "These are mega-superstar artists who, at the end of the day, have to learn how to sing duets. They're soloists. They have to figure out who's going to sing what, who comes in when, who's taking harmony, who's taking

Mariah Carey performs "I Still Believe" at the 1998 Billboard Music Awards. There she was recognized for having more number-one hit singles than any other female singer.

7

Mariah sings on stage with Australian singer Olivia Newton-John. Singing duets is rare for superstar artists who have created their own unique style.

lead vocal. . . . This is a once-in-a-lifetime lineup. This is lightning in a bottle. It will never happen again."

The concert was a benefit, meaning that the money raised from the event would go to charity. The event was organized by and televised on the music channel VH-1, which is part of a large corporation that also runs MTV, Nickelodeon, and TV Land. Many other corporations were anxious to help in this benefit concert including Blockbuster Video, Taco Bell, and Visa. Money from the "Divas Live" concert went to "Save the Music," a program designed to restore music education in public schools. Even before the concert, "Save the Music" had restored 91 musical programs, affecting 27,000 school children in New York City. Sponsors of "Save the Music" insist that children educated in music also develop better mentally and therefore perform better in their academic studies. The organizers of the program believe that music is good not only for the soul but also for the brain.

Mariah Carey was one of these believers. But, brain-boosting or not, she loved music and she could not remember a time when she did not. Mariah was the first of the five divas to perform in the "Divas Live" concert. The 28-year-old was certainly *the* diva of pop music. She had sold nearly half of the women's cumulative total of 200 million albums and claimed more than one dozen of the number-one hits.

Jennifer Aniston, the actress who plays Rachel on the hit TV show *Friends*, introduced the program. Then Mariah came on stage, strikingly beautiful at 5' 9" tall with long curly hair. Her wide, warm smile revealed her enthusiasm for the event. "How do you like the ensemble?" she asked the audience, twirling to show them her sleeveless, ankle-length dress. This show of pride in her shimmering gold gown broke the ice with the audience.

Mariah disliked singing one song and not being able to continue with her act, as she occasionally had to do for television shows like *The Tonight Show with Jay Leno* or *Late Show with David Letterman*. When that happened she felt that just as she was hitting her stride and really getting warmed up, her performance was over. Much to Mariah's delight, this concert was not so restricted. She would get to sing two songs back-to-back.

She began by singing "My All," one of her special favorites, or "faves," as she called them. She had written the lyrics after returning from a vacation in Puerto Rico. Walter Afanasieff, Mariah's song-writing partner, had helped Mariah compose this melody with rich Latin vibes. "My All" was described as "slinky, slow-jam R&B." This particular number-one hit was from *Butterfly*, her 1997 album that critics and many fans considered her most expressive. Near the end of "My All," she switched to a remix version, rearranging the song with a more hip-hop beat.

To sing her next song "Make It Happen," from her 1991 album *Emotions*, Mariah was joined by a choir. The song was a gospel with a funky Motown beat. Even though "Make It Happen" never made it to number one as a single, it was still very special to Mariah. She had written lyrics motivated by the most

Mariah Carey's childhood dream came true in April of 1998 at the "Divas Live" concert when she got to sing a duet with her idol Aretha Franklin, the "Queen of Soul."

painful memories of her past. But the song expressed her continuing faith as well:

> Not more than three short years ago
> I was abandoned and alone
> Without a penny to my name
> So very young and so afraid
> No proper shoes upon my feet
> Sometimes I couldn't even eat
> I often cried myself to sleep
> But still I had to keep on going
> Never knowing if I could take it
> If I could make it through the night
> I held on to my faith
> I struggled and prayed
> And now I've found my way . . .

Mariah remembered only too well her one pair of shoes: black lace-ups with holes in the soles. She also remembered her gnawing hunger, relieved only by a monotonous diet of macaroni and cheese. But she desperately wanted to encourage others and let them know how her faith sustained her. The lyrics came straight from her heart and soul. Mariah was drained when she finished singing "Make It Happen." But she was a shrewd performer too; with these two songs she had artfully showcased her singing by effortlessly transitioning through the styles of R&B, hip-hop, gospel, and Motown.

Although Gloria Estefan took the stage next, Mariah's singing was not over yet. Near the end of the concert she joined the other four divas and Carole King to sing King's classic song "Natural Woman." The concert ended with all of them singing "Testimony."

But Mariah's most thrilling moment of the entire concert came before that. In spite of all her honors and wealth it didn't seem possible she was singing a duet with Aretha Franklin— a version of Aretha's 1968 number-one hit "Chain of Fools." Aretha Franklin was a legend who had won an amazing 15 Grammy awards. Known as the "Queen of Soul," she had kept Mariah glued to the radio as a child. Mariah wasn't even born yet when Aretha recorded "Chain of Fools," so nothing made Mariah realize how far she had come in her own life more than singing onstage with a giant of the music world like Aretha Franklin.

2

CHILDHOOD REMEMBERED

M ariah was born on March 27, 1970, to Alfred and Patricia Carey. They lived on Long Island, a large island whose western end forms part of New York City. The southern part of the island boasts white-sand beaches. But the northern part—where Mariah's family lived near Huntington Bay—was hilly. The fact that her mother was a white woman of Irish descent and her father was a black man of Venezuelan descent meant little to Mariah in her early years. She did not realize her brother Morgan and her sister Alison, both older and already in school, were being teased about it. She did not understand why the family car was set on fire or why their pet dog was poisoned. Nor did she know what the words "racial discrimination" meant. But she did know that something made her mother and father argue. "There was always this tension," she said later. "They just fought all the time." It was about this time that Mariah acquired a lifelong habit of walking around on tiptoe.

But there was joy at home too. Mariah's mother Patricia,

Mariah Carey in a casual moment. As a child, Mariah amazed her family by singing opera at the age of three. By the time she was four years old she was taking voice lessons from her mother, singing scales, and immersed in the rigors of classical voice training.

a singer with the New York Opera, sang all day long. In fact, Mariah was born just as her mother's music career was taking off. When Mariah was still toddling around the house, her mother was practicing for the role of Maddalena, the sister of the villain, in the great opera *Rigoletto*. Mariah recalls how, even then, she could sense from her mother's voice—lowered from soprano to contralto— and her sly mannerisms that Maddalena was an evil character.

Although Maddalena appeared in only one act, the part was not easy. Maddalena was one of four characters who sing the famous song "Bella figlia dell amore," which means the "fairest daughter of the graces" in Italian. Because onstage two of the quartet sang inside the tavern and two sang outside its walls, perfect timing was essential. To get the timing right Patricia practiced to a recording. Once when her mother missed her cue, toddler Mariah sang her line—in Italian! "She wasn't yet three," remembered Patricia proudly.

Mariah seemed to absorb music like a sponge. Patricia did not talk down to her young daughter. Mariah wasn't denied "Sesame Street," but she also learned about musical terms such as sonority and consonance. At the dinner table, Mariah soon proved she was somewhat spoiled by the extra attention. Her father Alfred was very strict, insisting that his children speak only when spoken to. So Morgan and Alison were wide-eyed as toddler Mariah begin singing during dinner. Alfred banished her to the living room. But Mariah climbed up on a coffee table and warbled her song even louder. Alfred was not amused.

However, soon Alfred would leave the family.

Just one year later, Mariah's parents were divorced. Alfred took 12-year-old Alison to live with Mariah's grandmother and for a while he came to take Mariah for the weekends. Although the visits were very pleasant, they became fewer and farther between, and before long Mariah's father faded from her life.

Patricia had to work very hard now, trying to continue her opera career and giving voice lessons to make extra money. When Morgan was in school she had no choice but to take Mariah with her to work. It seemed only natural that she begin giving Mariah voice lessons too. At only four years old, Mariah was singing scales and doing all the things a singer does in classical voice training. She never thought it was unusual. Years later Mariah explained, "My mom always told me, 'You are special. You have a talent.'"

Patricia encouraged Mariah to sing snippets from opera and Broadway musicals. Mariah learned that her name had been inspired by the song "They Call the Wind Mariah" from the Broadway musical *Paint Your Wagon*. It was no surprise that at the age of six she easily won a part in a local production of the musical *South Pacific*. Dressed in a floppy sailor suit Mariah belted out the song "Honey Bun." Part of it ran:

A hundred and one pounds of fun
That's my little Honey Bun
Get a load of Honey Bun tonight
I'm speaking of my sweety pie
Only sixty inches high
Every inch is packed with dynamite
Her hair is blonde and curly
Her curls are hurly-burly. . .

Much tinier than 60" and 101 pounds,

A scene from the long-running Broadway musical Paint Your Wagon. *Mariah's name was taken from the majestic song "They Call the Wind Mariah," from that musical.*

Mariah danced and gestured to the simple lyrics. The lines were short and punchy. Best of all she got to play with the musical scale, showing off her range and talent by embellishing the words "tonight" and "dynamite." The audience enthusiastically applauded her. She could see huge grins on their faces and she felt as if she were bathed in love. It was the most wonderful feeling in the world for little Mariah.

However, much of the warmth in Mariah's childhood ended when she began school. There she was regarded as the lone "poor kid" in a well-to-do neighborhood. Some whispered that she wasn't like everyone else in another way. Although her hair was curly and dark blonde, her skin was very tan. Could she be the sister of that older girl Alison Carey? Everyone knew Alison was black. Mariah knew there was nothing wrong with being black, and she endured the stinging whispers.

There were times after school when Mariah did not feel entirely safe at home. Often her mother and Morgan weren't at home yet, so Mariah would go inside and lock the door behind her. Sometimes older kids stood outside throwing pebbles against the windows and taunting her. They quickly disappeared if Morgan showed up. Mariah also found relief another way. She would drown out her tormentors with the radio. "Beginning at age 7 . . . her only baby sitter was a little radio," wrote a newspaper reporter about Mariah after an interview some years later.

Although she loved all music on the radio, Mariah was most influenced by Morgan's favorite—soul music. She found herself seeking out the tunes of Aretha Franklin and Stevie Wonder, two giants of soul music. She was also intrigued by their successful careers. How did they start? How did they grow? What breakthroughs did they make?

Aretha had recorded many hits and was the originator of a style called "soul shouting." But in the mid-1970s Aretha reached out from soul and encompassed other musical forms, including pop, rock, gospel, blues, and R&B, or rhythm-and-blues.

Stevie Wonder lived up to his name. Being blind seemed irrelevant to his art. He began recording in 1963 at the age of 13. Within two years he was cranking out hit singles, most of which he wrote himself. He never seemed to

Mariah clowns around with the superstar recording artist Stevie Wonder, one of her childhood idols whose albums inspired her not only to write her own music but also to want to keep growing as an artist.

stop growing as an artist. Wonder was one of the first musicians to make albums that were not collections of singles but one whole musical statement. Perhaps more than anyone else, Stevie Wonder was the artist Mariah wanted to be like. Because she now knew she wanted to be a singing star, write her own music, and never stop growing as an artist.

Meanwhile Mariah listened, absorbed, and imitated her idols. "I used to take the radio from the kitchen and listen to it under the covers and sing all night," she recalled. She tried to imitate Minnie Ripperton, who hit unbelievable high notes in her song "Loving You."

Failure to duplicate Ripperton's feat just made Mariah more determined. Mariah also listened to Al Green and Gladys Knight. She soon realized soul music was derived from gospel music, so she explored gospel music too. She listened to the Clark Sisters, Shirley Caesar, Vanessa Bell Armstrong, and the incomparable Mahalia Jackson. Although Jackson had died when Mariah was only two years old, recordings preserved her extraordinarily deep, lively voice. Once Mariah saw a film of Mahalia singing. Never had she seen such depth of emotion in a singer's face. Mariah found that she soon loved gospel music too.

Later she said, "I love that style because it's so free and real and raw." Another time she admitted, "I get up and go to bed listening to gospel music." Mariah discovered that black gospel music was derived from spirituals and the field songs of African-American slaves.

But her taste was not limited to gospel and soul. As Mariah noted vocal techniques of various artists, she also gradually learned the origins of other forms of music. Soul and rock and roll were born of R&B. R&B was melded from two earlier forms: jazz and the blues. Somehow those two borrowed from ragtime and gospel. Rock and roll also borrowed from country music, both bluegrass and Nashville style. She continued to delve even deeper into music's origins. The more she learned, the more she knew she loved all aspects and forms of music. "Music makes me immeasurably happy," she gushed when she was older.

But Mariah knew that making it in the music business was hard. Her mother loved music too, and she had to struggle to survive.

3

THE MIRAGE

As hard as Mariah's mother had to work, she was sometimes home when Mariah got back from school. "I'd get home from school," Mariah recalled, "and she would have, like, five friends over who were jazz musicians, and I'd end up singing 'My Funny Valentine' at two in the morning."

Much of Mariah's childhood was spent as a little adult. She socialized with her mother and her mother's friends, listened lovingly to music, experimented with her singing, and even began to write poetry. Unfortunately, her sophisticated taste for poetry was not appreciated at school. Mariah's poetic effort in the third grade was rejected by the teacher, who complained that she must have copied it because it was so well written. Some of the teachers and other parents were prejudiced and had a low opinion of Mariah. "My mom was real permissive, so none of the parents wanted their kids to play with me. I was considered a bad influence," she recalled.

Rejection by children her own age hurt Mariah the most. In 1978, soon after Mariah turned eight, Morgan

Although she often felt rejected by other children, Mariah Carey found great happiness in music. While still a teenager, she developed a sophisticated singing style and was determined to make a life as an entertainer.

graduated from high school and left the family. Now Mariah and her mother were alone. Although they moved more than 10 times in the next nine years, Patricia Carey insisted they try to remain in the wealthier neighborhoods of Long Island. Among children her own age Mariah remained the poor kid of questionable origin. Although she could sing like an angel and even starred in the sixth-grade production of *The Sound of Music*, she still was not accepted by her peers. "Growing up, it was difficult for me to find people I connected with because of all my issues," she remembered later. But she had her mother and her other great love—music. Maria recalled thinking, "It was like 'These people may not think I'm as good as them, but I can *sing*!'"

By seventh grade, Mariah had made some friends. But she had also decided she was ugly. "I had all this frizzy hair and these bushy eyebrows," she said later. Her mother gave little instruction on how to improve her appearance. Mariah explained that her mother "wasn't one of those moms who dressed you up with little bows in your hair."

So Mariah took matters into her own hands. But instead of plucking her bushy eyebrows she shaved them off! Then, to make matters worse, in an attempt to make her hair over, she dyed it orange by accident. Except for a few friends, she had built a shell around herself. Because she was shunned by the popular kids no matter how well she performed, she pretended she was too cool to participate in school activities. "I thought I was the tough chick of the school," she remembered later, then admitted, "but I think that stemmed from being insecure."

Through her mother's love and her own love of music, she found peace. By now Mariah also had come to appreciate her voice as a complex, disciplined machine. She had learned her technique well: the diaphragm forces the lungs to expel air across the vocal chords; the sound resonates in the chest and mouth and is pitched and modulated by the tongue, lips, and teeth; and the sound is pure and resonating as well as projected. And Mariah knew there was still more to be discovered. Techniques such as tension and roughing yielded uniqueness to her voice. Devices for amplifying sound, like modern singers use, allowed her to use even more subtleties.

In seventh grade Mariah began to tell the world she was going to be a singer and a songwriter. Her handful of friends believed in her, but others at school did not. Mariah was not discouraged by their doubts and began to write songs. At the age of 14 she even looked for work as a singer. She sang so well that local recording studios gave her jobs singing backup and background rhythm for aspiring singers who wanted to make a demo. A demo is a recording made to demonstrate a singer's talents to recording companies. Mariah's limited success fueled her lofty ambitions even more. She explained to her mother why she didn't need to learn how to do housework. "I'm going to be a famous singer and have a maid."

Mariah's singing voice really wowed her brother Morgan. For her 16th birthday he paid for her to make her own demo, which she recorded in New York City on a professional 24-track system. At the recording studio a young musician named Ben Margulies was called in as a last-minute replacement for one of the instrumentalists. After the recording session Ben enthusiastically praised Mariah's range and expressiveness. He also revealed that he wanted to write music and was determined to do something about it. Ben's father owned a cabinet factory in New York City. Ben had set up a recording studio in a tiny back room in his father's factory where he intended to write and record songs. He was so taken by Mariah's singing that he immediately invited her to work with him in his studio. "[W]e sort of clicked as writers," said Mariah later.

Mariah saw Ben as a musical soulmate. She told him that she would like to write songs with him at his studio. First, however, she had to ask her mother if she could commute to New York City. The factory in which Ben had his studio was located in the Chelsea area of Manhattan, on the west side between the garment district to the north and Greenwich Village to the south. Just a few blocks north of the garment district was the theater district, home of glittery and legendary Broadway.

Luckily, Mariah's mother did not object to her commuting. "My mother was supportive and encouraging of my singing," Mariah later explained. As she travelled back and forth between Long Island and New York City to work with Ben, Mariah felt like she was now a part of the city. Often she did not get home until after midnight, and her attendance at Harborfield High School in Greenlawn suffered. She became known as the "mirage" because she was absent from school so often. Even when she made it to her classes, she usually had not completed her homework assignments. Her grades began to fall, and she was often summoned by a counselor.

"When you talked to her about it," remembered one counselor at the school, "she'd let you know it just wasn't that important in her life because she was going to be a rock star. She was fully convinced it was going to happen. Nothing was going to stand in her way. You could talk to her until you were blue in the face, and it didn't do any good."

The school officials were not at all pleased with what they believed to be her unrealistic ambitions. Counselors nudged Mariah into a

The sparkling lights of New York City attracted young Mariah. While still in high school she commuted from Long Island into New York City to write songs with Ben Margulies in his tiny makeshift studio. As soon as she graduated from high school, Mariah moved into the city.

vocational program. If she learned some kind of trade, at least she wouldn't starve, they said. So she consented to train as a beautician. In her high school years Mariah logged 500 hours learning how to use cosmetics and care for the skin and hair. All the while, in the evenings and on weekends, she and Ben wrote songs in his tiny makeshift studio. Ben said later of Mariah, "She had the ability just to hear things in the air and start developing songs out of them. Often I would sit down and start playing something, and from the feel of a chord she would start singing melody lines and coming up with a concept."

The first song the two recorded together was called "Here We Go Round Again." Mariah wrote the lyrics while Ben wrote the melody. With his synthesizer, Ben also made instrumental tracks. Mariah made several sound tracks, harmonizing her own voices. She was stunned at how wonderful the song sounded on their recording. She became even more determined to make a life in music. But that life had to be in New York City. She moved there in 1987, just days after graduating from Harborfield High. "I packed up my stuffed animals and my posters and tapes," said Mariah later, "and I moved into the city."

Mariah's mother did not object. She had also gone to the city when she was 17 years old. Life at home was no longer the same anyway. Mariah's mother had remarried, and her sister Alison had had a baby and was hooked on drugs. To support her habit Alison had become a prostitute. Alison seemed lost beyond hope, and she was only 25. Her sister's

Mariah on rollerskates mugging for the camera. Growing up in the company of her musical mother and her mother's musician friends, much of Mariah's childhood was spent as a little adult. Constantly working on and experimenting with her singing, at the age of 14 she worked at a local recording studio singing backup and background rhythm for other singers.

miserable life haunted Mariah. She had to do everything in her power to escape that same fate. Yet Mariah moved to Manhattan almost penniless with no job waiting for her.

4

ECHO IN THE CITY

Mariah moved into a small loft apartment in New York City with two other women her age. For 18 months she struggled. She finally got a few jobs singing backup, but the money was not enough to support her in an expensive city like New York. She fell farther and farther behind on her bills. She wore out her wardrobe item by item, including her last pair of shoes.

One Friday evening in November 1988 Mariah left her tiny apartment, locked the door, and walked down a flight of rickety stairs. She didn't want to go to the party that night hosted by Columbia Records. But Mariah had sung backup for R&B singer Brenda K. Starr, who was going to the party and had suggested that she come too. So Mariah waited inside the main door of her apartment building for Brenda to pick her up. Every few minutes she peeked out onto the noisy street and shivered. The night was chilly. "I waited, like, two hours for her, freezing," Mariah recalled.

Maria felt a bit foolish. She had put on her old high-school pep club jacket, and it certainly did not go with her bare-shouldered black dress. But it was the only

---

When she first moved to New York, Mariah Carey took jobs as a backup singer, and even as a floor sweeper in a beauty salon. After 18 months of struggling her demo tape finally opened the door to her commercial success.

warm coat she had. Mariah shrugged off feeling foolish. Singing backup was better than some of the jobs she had taken to survive. Being a waitress or a coat-checker wasn't bad, but the way the customers treated her was upsetting. She had lost some of those jobs for having "an attitude." But in her mind, it was the customers with the attitudes. Why did they think they could insult her because she served them? Her low point in employment was sweeping up hair clippings from the floor in a beauty salon. Mariah had to laugh as she remembered her phony name there: Echo.

"My demo tape!" she suddenly remembered. She fumbled in her purse. Yes, the demo tape cassette was there. She and Ben Margulies had labored long and hard in his studio to record their four very best songs. Mariah's voice could now range over seven octaves—almost the entire range of a piano. No one believed her when she said that. Even her doting mother doubted that remarkable range. But despite their disbelief, Mariah delighted in ending a line with a crescendo so high-pitched that all the dogs in New York City surely would have scattered in panic.

Brenda K. Starr finally came. Mariah wanted to complain about waiting so long, but she bit her tongue and went off to the party, with its usual disharmony of shrill voices that droned on hour after hour. However, eating tasty appetizers was a great improvement over the macaroni and cheese she existed on in her apartment. Even though Mariah knew her demo tape was good, she was embarrassed about approaching these well-dressed and well-paid executives with it.

Suddenly Mariah realized Brenda K. Starr had steered her into the presence of some Columbia Record executives. Should Mariah offer her tape? There was a man who caught her eye, one of several dark-suited, silk-tied men. Yet she hesitated to interrupt. Mariah remembered her thousands of hours of voice training and song writing. Her high-school pep club jacket never seemed more of a burden. Suddenly Brenda snatched the tape from her and offered it to the man. It seemed like a dream—in the midst of the clamor of voices—as the man reached out for Mariah's tape.

Out of nowhere another man snapped the tape out of Brenda's hand. "Great, another demo tape," he grumbled under his breath. "Thank you . . ." Mariah's voice trailed off as the man with the tape quickly wheeled around and disappeared into the crowd. The first man hadn't objected, so Mariah reasoned that they must both work for Columbia Records. She only hoped her tape wouldn't end up in the trash can somewhere. She had a sinking feeling that nothing would come of her efforts. If only they would listen to the tape, surely they would like the song "Someday."

Like so many of Mariah and Ben's songs "Someday" had been improvised. First they established a bass-and-drum line, then Mariah and Ben took off in soaring creative flight, which found itself in hip-hop. Once the lyrics and melody were solid, they added and mixed the tracks.

Later at her tiny apartment Mariah was sickened as she fretted over something else: had she written her name and phone number on the demo tape? For days this thought plagued her as she felt she had lost her big chance.

Monday morning there was a blunt message on Maria's answering machine. "I'm Tommy Mottola. Call me." The man gruffly added a telephone number. Mariah was sure that he was someone interested in offering her a waitressing job or maybe a backup gig. Wearily, she punched in the numbers on her phone. When a secretary answered, Mariah was informed that Tommy Mottola was an executive with Columbia Records. Abruptly a man's voice rumbled hello on the line.

Mariah heard herself stammering, "Can I speak to M-Mister M-Mottola?" After she got out his name, he barked, "I think we can make hit records." Mariah's mind raced wildly. She could scarcely hear Mottola explaining he was the man who took her demo tape at the party. Mariah had indeed forgotten to write down her name and phone number on the demo tape. It had taken him the whole weekend to track her down. Mariah felt like she was dreaming. But she forced herself to listen as Mottola invited her to his office that afternoon.

Her heart pounding rapidly, Mariah called her mother. There was no way she would talk to a record executive without her best friend. Patricia rushed into New York City from Long Island to meet Mariah when she heard the news. That afternoon Mariah felt as if she were sleepwalking and in a daze. With her mother's help Mariah found the Columbia Records building. She trembled deep inside as she presented herself to the secretary outside Tommy Mottola's office. Mariah became even more nervous when she learned that Mottola was president of the CBS Records Group, the company that owned Columbia Records. Now she was really frightened. For a moment she thought maybe this

whole thing was an elaborate practical joke.

But when she and her mother were ushered into Mottola's office, Mariah recognized him as the man at Friday's party, well-dressed and about 40 years old. He stood up and invited them to sit down. Mariah introduced her mother as the former opera singer she was. Mr. Mottola brazenly looked Mariah over. She wasn't foolish enough to object. She knew his stare was a professional appraisal. After all, a recording artist had to look good in videos. Tommy Mottola smiled approvingly, pleased that Mariah was as pretty as her soaring voice.

Mariah at a party with Tommy Mottola (left), who after listening to Mariah's first demo tape believed she was capable of making hit records. Mottola took the lead and helped to develop Mariah's early career with Columbia Records.

5

REACHING FOR GLORY

Mariah rarely had a moment to herself after her meeting with Tommy Mottola. A few days later she signed a contract with Columbia Records. At first she thought she would be free to produce an album with Ben Margulies, but she soon realized that would not be the case.

Mottola was fairly new at Columbia, and he had been hired to turn the company around. While Columbia Records had a stable of heavy-weight superstars, including Bruce Springsteen, Bob Dylan, the Rolling Stones, George Michael, Billy Joel, and Barbra Streisand, many of these artists were recording less and less. For the music industry the 1980s was the decade of female superstars like Whitney Houston. Yet Columbia Records did not have one active female superstar. That gossip made Mariah dizzy, for it was rumored that she was being groomed to be that star.

It seemed Mottola was telling everyone, "She's incredible; you just won't believe how good she is." Suddenly, fame frightened Mariah. She worried about losing the freedom she had had on her own. "I wasn't open to working

Mariah Carey with Tommy Mottola, who became her mentor, confidant, best friend, and husband.

with a superstar producer," Mariah admitted some time later.

Soon Mottola's strategy was unveiled. He turned Mariah over to promoter Don Ienner, the same promoter who had been at Arista Records and developed Whitney Houston's early career. Ienner was a proven starmaker. He began to line up high-powered producers to develop Mariah. Recruits Rick Wake, Rhett Lawrence, and Narada Michael Walden had worked with stars like Smokey Robinson, Michael Jackson, and Whitney Houston.

Lost in the tornado of activity was Ben Margulies. As if to console him, Mariah got together with him before the producers arrived. The two composed and recorded a new song called "Vision of Love." With this song added to a 12-song demo, Mariah hoped to make sure some of their songs got on an album.

Mariah was pleased when "Vision of Love" excited the three new producers. They said they were impressed with all the songs she and Ben had written, but they insisted on some rear-ranging. Each producer also began to develop his own material with Mariah. The very first day she met with Rick Wake in New York they wrote "There's Got To Be A Way." She developed a gospel-like crying ballad called "I Don't Wanna Cry" with Narada Michael Walden.

Mariah had to fly to Los Angeles to work with Rhett Lawrence, with whom she wrote "You Need Me" and "Sent From Up Above." Rhett also changed "Vision of Love." He took it from what he called "a fifties sort of shuffle" to a more up-tempo danceable song. He went on to add guitars and bass to the drums of Mariah and Ben's original arrangement.

Month after month Mariah worked on songs for the album, flying from studios in New York to Los Angeles. Sometimes she felt that her strong voice was overpowered by the backup instrumentals. But a waitress/coat-check girl/ backup singer was not about to complain to professionals who had worked with the likes of Michael Jackson and Whitney Houston.

Mottola insisted the album be perfect. The video of the most promising single, "Vision of Love," was especially important to get right. A superb video shown on MTV and VH-1 would have an enormous impact on the success of a new album. Yet when Mottola was shown the finished video of "Vision of Love," he didn't like it at all and ordered it scrapped. The remaking of the new video was rumored to have cost more than half a million dollars. "If it costs a few extra dollars to make a splash in terms of the right imaging, you go ahead and do it," Don Ienner said defensively.

Envious people gossiped that Mariah was getting favors she didn't deserve. But Rhett Lawrence, who had worked with megastar Michael Jackson, said the first time he heard Mariah sing, "I literally got goose bumps on my arms." After Rick Wake first heard Mariah he said, "It was obvious that she was great." Mariah tried to ignore the negative gossip. She knew these accomplished producers in the music world would not praise her if she didn't deserve it.

By early 1990 the album was almost finished. Simply called *Mariah Carey,* it delivered 11 songs, six written by Mariah and Ben Margulies. Ben would get some glory from the album if it was successful. The album dedication read "To my sister Alison—keep shining." Mariah also

Mariah Carey on tour. Her high-energy 1990 tour took her and her troupe to nine cities and showcased her first album.

thanked those who helped her on the album. At the top of list was "God, for the precious gift of music that brings me immeasurable joy," followed by Tommy Mottola, Mom, Ben, Brenda K., Morgan, and several other individuals who helped produce the album.

In spring 1990, even before the album was released, Mariah was introduced to the public. Mottola had organized a nine-city tour to showcase her talent for radio managers and record store buyers. The buyers at a convention going on in Los Angeles were the first to hear Mariah perform live. "The energy level in that room was astounding," said one buyer after the session with Mariah.

By the time she finished the brief tour, Mariah had hit her stride. She was sensational. Mariah sang "America the Beautiful" in Detroit at the opening game of the National Basketball Association championship playoffs. She also appeared on *The Arsenio Hall Show* and *The Tonight Show with Jay Leno*. When someone told her *Mariah Carey* was being promoted harder than any first album since Bruce Springsteen's first album 15 years before, she was amazed.

Then Columbia released her album, and by early August it topped the *Billboard* charts at number one, while at the same time "Vision of Love" was the number-one single. Not only did thousands of copies of *Mariah Carey* sell every day, but three individual songs from the album —"Love Takes Time," "Someday," and "I Don't Wanna Cry"—followed "Vision of Love" to become number-one singles. The album quickly went platinum, meaning a million copies had been sold. It soon rushed on to multiple platinum. Success was due in great part to the managerial genius of Tommy Mottola and Don Ienner, but most importantly, it was a result of the commitment and musical genius of Mariah Carey.

Critics raved about Mariah's voice with phrases like "powerhouse style, soaring from low growl to an ethereal wail," "purring alto to stratospheric," "a voice that can probably shatter glass and then put it back together," and "a riveting seven-octave roller coaster of sound."

Fans wait for hours outside Tower Records in New York City in lines that stretch around the block for an opportunity to have Mariah Carey's signature on one of her CDs. Mariah's first album went platinum just a few weeks after its release.

Mariah left her tiny loft apartment and moved into a luxurious 21st-floor apartment on the posh Upper East Side of New York City. At last she seemed able to indulge in luxuries. Mariah loved animals, so soon her apartment was home for two beautiful Persian cats, Ninja and Tompkins, and a tiny Yorkshire Terrier named Ginger. She decorated the walls with giant posters of two tragic stars of the past, Marilyn Monroe and James Dean. Before her big break, Mariah had once considered herself somewhat tragic too, but the success of her album and her unbelievable string of number-one singles changed that. She now seemed to be the luckiest person in the world.

However, she still worked harder than ever. She made videos for singles as they emerged on the charts and endured reporters by the dozens. Over and over Mariah had to answer the same questions. Yes, her favorite color was pink, although she liked to wear black. Yes, she loved animals. Her dress size was 6. Her idols were Stevie Wonder and Aretha Franklin. Yes, she favored pasta and salad. She liked to watch comedy or horror movies. She had no middle name. Yes, she adored the beach. She even admitted she thought the right side of her face was more attractive than the left side.

But few reporters were happy with the facts; they wanted some sensational news.

6

CINDERELLA DAYS

S ome reporters tried to goad Mariah into saying she was not recording the kind of music she really loved. Some tried to get her to admit her relationship with Tommy Mottola was more than business. They pried into her past. Her childhood of hardship was a badge of honor for her. But it also held some tragic secrets, like her sister Alison's problems with drugs and prostitution. Once she led a reporter to believe she had only one sibling, her brother Morgan.

As always, the subject of race came up. The answer that she was both white and black didn't please reporters. It was as if she had to pick one or the other. Once she answered testily that she was tri-racial. Technically that was correct because her Venezuelan father also had Indian blood. "I am a human being, a person. . . . If people enjoy my music, then they shouldn't care what I am, so it shouldn't be an issue," she explained in frustration.

Despite all of the questions, Mariah's life was heavenly. In 1990 she was nominated for five coveted Grammy Awards. In February 1991, at Radio City Music Hall in

---

Mariah's initial success brought fame, along with reporters investigating her personal life, past and present, and digging for sensational news.

New York City, she won two—one for Best New Artist and one for Best Female Pop Vocal. She also sang "Vision of Love" during the ceremonies. Just one month later she was in Los Angeles to accept three Soul Train Awards for the R&B/Urban division: Best New Artist, Best Album by a Female, and Best Single by a Female. She also won *Rolling Stone* magazine's Readers' Pick for Best New Singer.

Mariah's career was sizzling hot. Sadly her writing partnership with Ben Margulies ended over a legal dispute. Her new partner was Walter Afanasieff. The two worked the same way she and Ben had. Walter would play chords on the keyboard and Mariah would respond with a wordless melody. The two would then collaborate into making a musical score. Then Mariah would create the words or lyrics. Carole King, who wrote "Natural Woman," also partnered with Mariah to write "If It's Over."

Mariah spent most of her time now working in the studio on her next album. Few artists are able to follow up one album with another within a year. Albums are difficult to produce because they have to be a unified statement and not a hodgepodge of different themes. With the help of her producers and by her own unstinting hard work, Mariah created her second album, *Emotions,* by August 1991.

Emotions was a strong follow-up album. Mariah had insisted on less backup and a more R&B sound, although the album was still basically dance/R&B/ballad like her debut album. By October the single "Emotions" had reached number one, giving Mariah an unprecedented five straight number-one singles. She just missed her sixth number-one single when "Can't Let Go," stalled at number two. But it

was becoming clear in the record industry that she might join the ranks of the greatest recording artists who ever lived, up there with her idols Aretha Franklin and Stevie Wonder, as well as Elvis and the Beatles. All of her success had happened in a period of three years— Mariah was just 21 years old.

Despite her record-selling success, Mariah made few personal appearances and rarely performed publicly. Everyone wondered when she would tour, but Mariah had spent so much time in studios that the thought of performing

Mariah Carey had reason to smile at the 1991 Grammy Awards at Radio City Music Hall, where she was nominated for five Grammy Awards and won two. Mariah also entertained the audience when she sang her number-one hit "Vision of Love" during the ceremonies.

before the public scared her. Still she was determined to get over this fear and dispel the rumor that her music was manufactured by sound engineers.

In early 1992 she got a chance to perform in public without exhausting herself on a tour. She decided to perform on "MTV Unplugged," a very popular television program. For three years she had been backed up by her own voice, synthesizers, and drum machines. Now she would perform with real singers and musicians.

On March 16, 1992, in New York City, Mariah went onstage dressed in all black: jeans, leotard top, short jacket, and boots. She was accompanied by four strings, five horns, drums, bass, guitar, piano, and ten singers. The musicians and singers backed her up in various combinations. She wanted a vocally driven performance. She began with "Emotions," followed by "If It's Over" and "Make It Happen." The highlight of the show was her rendition of the old Jackson Five hit, "I'll Be There." By June 1992 "I'll Be There" gave Mariah her sixth number-one single.

After her virtuoso performance no one thought Mariah was manufactured in a studio. She was truly reigning as Queen of Pop. Her only real competition, Whitney Houston, was solidly into movies now. Whitney had not released any new albums since *I'm Your Baby Tonight* in 1990.

As much as she enjoyed sharing her gift with an audience, Mariah soon discovered one of the downsides to being a superstar. Many celebrities are sued for false reasons, just in the hope they will make settlement payments in order to avoid bad publicity, and Mariah was now a target. The worst lawsuit came from Mariah's stepfather. He and Mariah's mother were separated, and divorce seemed certain. He sued Mariah, claiming he had supported her in the expectation of sharing her eventual income. Mariah insisted that was untrue. There were also several additional lawsuits stemming from songwriters who claimed she had stolen their songs.

Mariah found some consolation in the fact that her real father had not taken any advantage of her fame and wealth. He may have become distant, but he was not a hypocrite. Later she reflected in admiration, "[H]e is the one person in my life . . . that never asked me for anything." On another occasion she said, "He has not come out of the woodwork saying stupid things about me. . . . He's a good person."

When the public found out she was involved with Tommy Mottola, Mariah really became a lightning rod. Mottola had recently divorced, so reporters speculated Mariah had broken up his marriage. Since he was her boss, reporters also speculated Mariah's success was due to her romantic involvement with him. Reporters also hinted that she didn't really write songs and that she was given credit only because Mottola insisted on it. Writing nasty articles about Mariah became very fashionable, but she tried not to let them bother her.

The truth was that Mariah *was* smitten with Tommy Mottola. Whereas her mother had once been her mentor, her confidante, her protector, and her best friend, Tommy now filled those roles and more. She lived for music, and Tommy knew music as few others did. He was a man of the world too, much more interesting and traveled than men Mariah's own age. He entertained her dreams of a huge mansion on a vast estate with horses and other pets. And he

When Mariah married Tommy Mottola, he helped to fulfill her wildest dreams, including moving them into a spectacular mansion on an estate filled with horses and dogs—Mariah's favorite pets.

offered her an honest relationship: marriage. Many young performers—actresses, singers, figure skaters—marry their older mentors, and Mariah was happy to share both her professional and personal lives with the same man.

"It just sort of happened," she explained. "Tommy is just the greatest person. He knows so much; he's funny. I can't imagine anybody else who would be so supportive and so understanding and helpful. He lifts me up. . . .

Everybody who knows us realizes that we're right for each other."

Her Cinderella life continued. When she was not recording her next album she was planning her wedding, which she modeled after the 1981 royal wedding of Prince Charles of England and Lady Diana Spencer. After months of planning, the wedding finally took place June 5, 1993, at St. Thomas Episcopal Cathedral in New York City. Among the 300 invited guests were Mariah's family, including her father, and celebrities such as Gloria Estefan, Bruce Springsteen, Robert DeNiro, Billy Joel, Tony Danza, and Barbra Streisand. Security police reportedly numbered 200.

Mariah walked down the aisle in a pale ivory, off-the-shoulder gown with a beaded bodice designed by Vera Wang. On her head was a tiara trailed by an English tulle veil sparkling with small stones. Her gown's 27-foot train was born by six bridesmaids. After the ceremony 47 flower girls showered Mariah and Tommy with rose petals. Reporters speculated the wedding cost half a million dollars, marveling that her satin pumps alone cost $1,000.00. Their estimate didn't include her six-carat, pear-shaped diamond engagement ring.

All Mariah could say later was, "When I look back and think about it, it's so unbelievable! I mean, it really is like Cinderella."

For five years she had been blessed and her good fortune showed no sign of stopping.

7

ALWAYS GROWING

Shortly after their Hawaiian honeymoon, Mariah and Tommy returned to their lavish high-rise apartment in New York City, and Mariah's new album *Music Box* came out. In this album Mariah attempted to suppress her vocal pyrotechnics. Critics judged her performance too laid back, too cool. Many of the songs lacked passion, they said. The result disappointed few of her fans, though. The album sold well and yielded two more number-one hits, "Hero" and "Dreamlover." Mariah now had an astonishing eight number ones, and she had sold millions of each of her four albums. However, Mariah did not just want money, she also wanted to grow as an artist, and finally she was going to answer charges that she could not tour.

She later remembered her first live concert in Miami with dread. "I had to walk up this ramp onto the stage and I heard this deafening scream and it was kinda like everything in my life, this whole incredible whirlwind I'd been going through, it had all been leading up to that insane moment—and there I was."

Mariah Carey performing live. Her first live concert in Miami filled her with dread, but her next concerts went well, proving to herself and others that she could tour successfully.

The huge Miami Arena was made of con-
crete, so sound bounced off the walls and then
reverberated a series of echoes back at Mariah.
Nevertheless, she felt she performed well. To
her astonishment a few critics trashed the
performance. Television news jumped on the
bad reviews, reporting she had failed. Mariah
suppressed the feeling she was being wronged.
She just worked harder to prepare for her next
concert near Boston. She was going to make
sure no critic would dare say she had not suc-
ceeded. It worked. The *Boston Globe* hailed her
concert there as spectacular. Mariah explained,
"I didn't come up doing clubs like most people,
so I wasn't ready." She added with great satis-
faction, "Now I am."

Mariah triumphantly finished her tour. She
had added another dimension to her career
and now decided to back off her hectic sched-
ule. Her one recording effort for 1994 was a
Christmas album.

During her time off she became involved in
the Fresh Air Fund. The program gives underprivileged New York City kids an opportunity to
experience the outdoors. Each summer the
Fresh Air Fund gives about 3,000 children the
chance to hike, canoe, swim, and fish at five
camps north of the city. Besides having fun,
the kids develop self-esteem and leadership
skills. Mariah pledged $1 million and she fre-
quently visits the summer camps. Because of
her generosity, one of the camps is now called
Camp Mariah.

Not far from Camp Mariah is the town of
Bedford, New York, where Tommy and Mariah
purchased a 65-acre estate in forested hills
and lush pastures. Mariah enthusiastically

began decorating the interior of their huge hill-top mansion. She also added horses, including a palomino named Misty, cats Ninja and Tompkins, and a pack of devoted dogs that included Ginger and a fireball terrier named Jack. "I'm this poor kid from Long Island and now—this!" marveled Mariah. "I couldn't have made it any better if I'd created it myself."

Mariah enjoyed her life as a wealthy princess of pop. She still recorded in studios and occasionally granted interviews. In one interview Mariah said, "Most people—especially women—have to go through years of working with men who tell them what to do and write all the songs and produce everything and the women just sit back and sing. I never wanted to

Mariah with children at the Fresh Air Fund's Camp Mariah. She has contributed substantial financial support to the program, which gives underprivileged New York City children a chance to experience the outdoors each summer.

Mariah Carey rehearses with Boyz II Men. Her single, "One Sweet Day," performed with the group, rocketed to number one on the singles charts when it was released in 1996.

do that. Even before I got my record deal I had a lot of songs."

But in fact Tommy Mottola seemed more and more controlling. He criticized clothing Mariah wore and told her she shouldn't listen to rap. He told her professionally he did not want her to get into hip-hop, urban music that is a cross between rap and R&B. His control was never more evident than when Mariah ventured from the Bedford estate or the New York apartment and Mottola had someone follow her. Mariah began to feel like a prisoner. It seemed bizarre that a 24-year-old woman who had earned millions of dollars was not really free.

She threw herself into her next album *Daydream*. She defied Tommy and did go hip-hop on some songs. *Daydream* was praised for its strong selection of songs, and Mariah was praised for her passion. "One Sweet Day," a song that she performed with Boyz II Men, took off as a single and clinched the top spot on the charts. So did "Fantasy" and "Always Be My Baby." Mariah now had an astonishing 11 number-one singles. She had also sold a mind-boggling 80 million albums.

With *Daydream* Mariah became adventurous with remixes and performing with other singers. The music world liked her new directions, much the same way she had always admired the versatility of Stevie Wonder. Mariah wanted to make yet another move—one that Tommy Mottola strongly opposed. She wanted to act in movies. Soon Mariah and Tommy argued more and more. The public did not learn the details of their feud, but by the end of 1996 Mariah and Tommy had separated.

In early 1997 Mariah began taking acting lessons and working on songs for a new album called *Butterfly*. Hip-hop and rap producer Sean "Puffy" Combs became involved in the album. Mottola may have disapproved, but as kingpin of Columbia Records he did not interfere. After its release in mid-1997, *Butterfly*

Mariah Carey and Whitney Houston perform their Oscar-nominated song, "When You Believe," at the 1999 Academy Awards ceremony. Mariah has even surpassed such greats as Whitney and her childhood idol Aretha Franklin with the most number-one songs by any female soloist in history.

gained Mariah many new fans and satisfied her older ones as well. Many critics liked the edgier urban sound of *Butterfly.* The single "Honey" rushed to number one, giving Mariah the most number-one songs by any female soloist in history.

The video of "Honey," showing Mariah escaping from a gangster, caused quite a stir. Many thought that it represented Mariah escaping from Tommy Mottola. Not long thereafter, "My All" reached number one. After their separation, when Mottola was asked how he felt about Mariah's success, he graciously responded, "Mariah is a world-class superstar, and I remain her biggest fan."

Mariah also remained cordial toward Tommy in public. Of Tommy's controlling nature she said, "When you've experienced more than someone else, it's a natural tendency to try to protect the other person from the things that you've gone through." Then she added, "But now, I have to learn things for myself. I have to experience things for myself. I have to make my own decisions and live by them."

By early 1998 Mariah and Tommy had divorced. She firmed up her acting plans by being cast in several films. The first film is a comedy called *The Bachelor* with Chris O'Donnell. Another scheduled film is a spy spoof called *Double-O-Soul* in which Mariah shares the big screen with comedian Chris Tucker. Another movie, *All That Glitters*, is being developed especially as a showcase for Mariah, whose star continues to burn bright and strong.

CHRONOLOGY

1970	Born on March 27 to Patricia and Alfred Carey in Long Island, New York.
1973	Parents separate; Mariah and older brother Morgan remain with their mother, sister Alison leaves with their father.
1986	Begins commuting to New York City to write music with Ben Margulies.
1987	Graduates from Harborfield High School and moves to New York City.
1988	Meets Tommy Mottola; signs contract with Columbia Records.
1990	Is introduced to the public with a nine-city tour; first album entitled *Mariah Carey* is released, goes platinum, and hits number one on the *Billboard* charts; four singles from the album hit number one; nominated for five Grammy Awards.
1991	Wins two Grammy Awards; second album is released; the single "Emotions," from the album, hits number one.
1992	Performs on *MTV Unplugged;* "I'll Be There" becomes her sixth number-one single.
1993	Marries Tommy Mottola; fourth album *Music Box* is released; two more singles hit number one.
1994	Tours; album *Merry Christmas* is released.
1995	Releases *Daydream*; gets involved with Fresh Air Program; produces two more number-one singles.
1996	Separates from Tommy Mottola.
1997	Releases album *Butterfly*; divorces Tommy Mottola; begins taking acting lessons.
1998	Named the female singer with the most number-one singles of all time when "My All" hits number one to become her thirteenth; sings duet with Whitney Houston; wins Oscar Award for "When You Believe."
1999	Album sales approach 100 million; appears in the movie *The Bachelor* with Chris O'Donnell.

ACCOMPLISHMENTS

Albums

1990	*Mariah Carey*
1991	*Emotions*
1992	*MTV Unplugged*
1993	*Music Box*
1994	*Merry Christmas*
1995	*Daydream*
1997	*Butterfly*
1998	*Number Ones*

Number-One Singles

1990	"Vision of Love," "Love Takes Time"
1991	"Someday," "I Don't Wanna Cry," "Emotions"
1992	"I'll Be There"
1993	"Dreamlover," "Hero"
1995	"Fantasy," "One Sweet Day"
1996	"Always Be My Baby"
1997	"Honey"
1998	"My All"

Videos/Movies

1991	*Mariah Carey: The First Vision* (video)
1992	*MTV Unplugged + 3* (video)
1993	*Mariah Carey* (video), *Fantasy* (video)
1999	*The Bachelor* (movie), *Double-O-Soul* (movie, tentative)
2000	*All That Glitters* (movie, tentative)

MAJOR U.S. AWARDS

1990   Three "Soul Train" Awards

1991   Two Grammy Awards—Best Pop Vocal and Best New Artist

1991–96 Six American Music Awards; six Billboard Music Awards

1994   Two Rockefeller Center Awards

1999   Congressional Humanitarian Award; NAACP Image Award

ABOUT THE AUTHOR

SAM WELLMAN lives in Kansas. He has degrees from colleges in the Midwest and the Ivy League. He has written a number of biographies of notable people—as diverse as George Washington Carver, Mother Teresa, Billy Graham, and Michelle Kwan—for both adults and younger readers.

FURTHER READING

Cox, Ted. *Whitney Houston*. Philadelphia: Chelsea House Publishers, 1998.

Davis, Sheila. *The Craft of Lyric Writing*. Cincinnati, Ohio: Writers Digest Books, 1985.

Erlewine, Michael, and others (eds). *All Music Guide to Rock*. 2nd ed. San Francisco: Miller Freeman Books, 1997.

George, Nelson. *Hip Hop America*. New York: Viking Press, 1998.

Gourse, Leslie. *Aretha Franklin: Lady Soul*. New York: Franklin Watts, 1995.

Graff, Gary, and others (eds). *Musichound R&B: The Essential Album Guide*. Detroit: Visible Ink Press, 1997.

Miller, Richard. *The Structure of Singing*. New York: Schirmer Books, 1986.

Nickson, Chris. *Mariah Carey Revisited*. New York: St. Martin's Griffin, 1998.

Schmidt, Jan. *Basics of Singing*. New York: Schirmer Books, 1998.

Webb, Jimmy. *Inside the Art of Songwriting*. New York: Hyperion, 1998.

Wolfe, Charles K. *Mahalia Jackson, Gospel Singer*. Philadelphia: Chelsea House Publishers, 1990.

INDEX